Original title:
Life: Full of Questions, No Answers

Copyright © 2025 Creative Arts Management OÜ
All rights reserved.

Author: Oliver Bennett
ISBN HARDBACK: 978-1-80566-257-0
ISBN PAPERBACK: 978-1-80566-552-6

Sounds of the Skeptic Heart

What's up with the sun? Is it hot, or just shy?
Clouds always look grumpy, floating on high.
Do birds have a gossip? Oh, what do they share?
I wonder if trees ever cut their own hair.

Do cats see in color or just think we're dull?
Is a goldfish's bowl a vast ocean full?
Do echoes get tired of repeating our chat?
Why do I ask questions when I'm busy with that?

Why does a perky dog always chase his own tail?
Is the moon just a pebble in an enormous scale?
Do ants hold a meeting when we're not around?
Or do they just hop and stomp — too loud to be found?

Perhaps squirrels barter for the best nutty spot?
While raccoons discuss who eats leftovers hot.
I keep asking 'why' as I sip my green tea,
But maybe the fun's in the mystery spree!

Where the Mind Wanders

In the fridge, I search for truth,
But find only old, forgotten youth.
I ponder cheese and yogurt's fate,
Are they still fresh, or just second rate?

Chasing shadows with my trusty pen,
I write down thoughts like 'Where's my zen?'
But they vanish faster than my socks,
Leaving me talking to old clocks.

Fragments of the Unseen

I met a cat who knew it all,
But when I asked, it took a fall.
Its wisdom, like a feather tossed,
Just left me laughing, slightly lost.

A bowl of noodles holds their secrets,
But they just slurp, don't care for regrets.
I ask them, 'What's the meaning here?'
They twirl my thoughts, then disappear.

The Weight of Wonder

I tried to weigh my worries down,
But ended up with just a frown.
A scale won't hold my endless thoughts,
It seems they play like silly knots.

Why's my toast always land buttered side?
Maybe it's answering things I've denied.
The universe laughs, I swear I heard,
As I spilled coffee, not a word!

Searching for the Unreachable

I searched for answers in a donut hole,
But found only crumbs, that took a toll.
A sprinkle of joy and sugar on top,
Yet questions remain, never to stop.

I tried to catch the moon with a net,
But it giggled and made me forget.
Stars twinkled down like they knew the spree,
As I looked up, feeling quite free.

Uncharted Waters of Wonder

Riding waves of thought at play,
With riddles tossed like seaweed sway.
Is the moon made of cheese or just light?
Surfing through dreams that take flight.

Fish laugh as they form a crew,
Telling tales that aren't quite true.
Why do socks disappear in the wash?
A mystery that makes me say, 'Gosh!'

The Art of Uncertainty

Painting clouds with a twist of fate,
Unraveling yarn, but isn't it great?
Why do we ponder while we binge our shows?
A riddle wrapped in popcorn, who knows?

Waltzing with doubts on a rainy day,
Quirky thoughts at play, come what may.
If time flies, can I catch a ride?
Or just watch it zoom like a roller coaster glide?

Tapestries of Thought

Weaving dreams with a thread of jest,
Stitching questions that never rest.
Is coffee a hug in a porcelain cup?
Or just a jolt to wake me up?

Knitting patterns of sheer surprise,
With every stitch, another why lies.
Who decided that cats were the best?
While dogs just bark and take a rest?

Constellations of Ignorance

Stars twinkle with mischief tonight,
Whispering secrets of sheer delight.
If a tree falls, does it make a sound?
Or just giggles echoing all around?

Galaxies spin in a dance of cheer,
As questions float like a nice cold beer.
Why do we park in driveways, pray?
Life's quirky maze, come what may!

The Weight of Unasked Prayers

I tossed my hopes on a wishing star,
They fell like socks, both near and far.
The mailbox filled with absent replies,
Is anyone out there? Just empty skies!

I asked my cat for a bit of advice,
He stared at me like I'm not so nice.
With wisdom like that, I'm left in the lurch,
Guess I'll just hope, and start a new search.

Mirage of Clarity on the Horizon

I squinted hard at the bright sun's glare,
Is that a mirage, or just hot air?
I wave my hands like a crazy mime,
Still lost in thoughts that won't stand in line.

Maps are great, till you get them wet,
I think I'll stick with my vague mindset.
Round and round in this dusty heat,
Finding answers feels like a real defeat.

Insomniac Musings Under the Moon

Moonlight whispers, the night is long,
My brain is a theater, with no clear song.
Counting sheep just leads to more sheep,
What was I pondering? It's gone, no leap!

A ghost of a thought, it waltzes away,
Where it's off to, who's to say?
Insomnia's a friend, or maybe a foe,
I laugh with the stars, as they steal the show.

Beneath the Surface of Knowing

I dove for wisdom in the deep blue sea,
Found a rubber fish, said, "What's next for me?"
It flopped and floundered, a dance so absurd,
What made me think answers could be heard?

A scholar once told me to seek my truth,
But all I found was my old lost tooth.
So here I am with this riddle and jest,
Maybe not knowing is truly the best.

Stars Beyond the Questions

Twinkling lights in the sky so bright,
Who knew they'd spark my sleepless night?
Why do they dance, why do they glow?
Maybe they laugh at the things we don't know.

Each star a question, a riddle to solve,
But my brain's in knots, problems evolve.
I shout at the moon, 'Can you give me a clue?'
It winks back, 'Kid, I'm puzzling too!'

A Road Without Signs

Driving fast down a road so wide,
No signs to guide, just questions to ride.
Is this the way to my dreams, or fears?
Will I laugh or will I burst into tears?

Round every bend, a mystery awaits,
Confusion completely mistaken for fate.
"Is that a landmark?" I ask my phone,
It rolls its eyes, "You're still alone!"

Starlit Queries

In the night sky, questions abound,
Do aliens laugh at the sounds we've found?
I wonder if clouds hold secrets untold,
Or just fluffy fluff that gets old and cold.

Every twinkle's a giggle, a tease from afar,
Asking if we're lost, or if we are stars.
So I dance with the moon, and pirouette with the breeze,
Trying to solve the riddle of how to say 'cheese!'

The Weight of Whimsy

With a pocketful of whimsy and a heart full of cheer,
I walk through the questions that jump out of fear.
What if the clouds can't hold back their rain?
Would I float like a feather or wag my complaint?

And if socks could talk, what stories they'd share,
About adventures in washing machines, oh so rare!
Giggles and chuckles, the answers we seek,
Might just be hiding in the fun and the freak!

Hazy Skies of Reflection

Clouds wear hats, oh what a sight,
As birds debate in mid-flight.
The sun plays hide and seek all day,
While I just sip my tea, hooray!

Should I wear socks with shoes today?
Or is it cooler to let them sway?
The breeze just laughs and rolls its eyes,
As I question the meaning of blue skies.

Sometimes I ponder, why does toast fall?
And is there method in my small brawl?
If cats could talk, what would they say?
Do they judge my style in every way?

In this dance of thoughts, I twirl around,
Spinning with whims that know no ground.
The answers hide just out of reach,
Yet I'm entertained by each new breach.

Beyond the Nest of Certainty

Chickens scratch and cluck with glee,
While pondering deep philosophy.
Do eggs feel safe within their shell?
Or are they itching to break the spell?

A squirrel ponders nuts each fall,
Calculating risks, after all.
Do cats dream of chasing dust?
Or do they think they simply must?

The sun and moon dance in such flair,
While I just stare and scratch my hair.
If cheese could talk, what tales it'd tell,
Of sandwiches bold and the toasty smell!

Around and around my thoughts do spin,
Seeking answers but can't win.
Maybe it's fun to question all,
And just enjoy this cosmic ball.

Whims of the Wandering Mind

A bumblebee buzzes, lost in thought,
Wondering why it's so heavily sought.
Does it know the flowers are on its case?
Or is it just searching for its place?

The toaster sighs, why's no one around?
Waiting for toast, it makes a sound.
If only muffins would come to play,
Would they chat about the weather all day?

In shadows, I ask, do spoons have moods?
Are they ever tired of their food broods?
And when I laugh, does the moon chuckle back?
Or does it keep secrets in its silver stack?

Funny how wonders dance in my head,
Like socks in the dryer, unpaired and spread.
Maybe questions spin out of fright,
And in the chaos, we find delight.

Questions Underneath the Surface

Fish swim by with knowing smirks,
Do they ponder life's little quirks?
Is there water in space, oh dear?
Or do stars just giggle, never near?

A dog rolls by, chasing its tail,
In a cosmic quest, it will prevail!
Do they ever think of the postman's scent?
Or is it just treats that they represent?

Trees gossip softly, rustling leaves,
Are they judging us while we breathe?
What do they know of wind and rain?
Or do they just dance to ease the strain?

In my tangled mind, questions collide,
While laughter echoes from deep inside.
Isn't it funny to drift and roam,
Inquirers searching for a cozy home?

The Ocean of the Unexplained

Why does the toaster burn the bread?
My socks always vanish, are they wed?
Is coffee just beans on a swirl?
Or a potion to make life unfurl?

Why do cats stare like they know?
What secrets do they keep, oh so slow?
Is the fridge a portal to another dimension?
Or just the keeper of leftovers' retention?

Where do the wrinkles come from at night?
Is it just laughter or a pillow fight?
Do birds have a club where they plot?
Or do they just chill and forget what they thought?

Why do we chase, yet stand still?
Is there a map to our heart's thrill?
The ocean's vast yet we still wade,
In a sea of thoughts, forever portrayed.

Footprints in the Fog

Why do my shoes leave marks in the mist?
Were they dancing or summoning a twist?
If fog could talk, what tales would it spin?
Or would it just giggle, saying, 'Where have you been?'

What's the secret behind the stray cat's stare?
Does it ponder the mysteries of the air?
Are shoes supposed to always be matched?
Or does chaos create styles that are hatched?

Why does the cereal always get soggy?
Is it the milk that gets a little foggy?
Do the clouds ever use a GPS?
Or are they too lost to even guess?

In a world where questions never cease,
Perhaps laughter is the best kind of peace.
So let's skip in the fog with silly delight,
And ponder the nonsense till the morning light.

Whirlwind of Wonders

Why do socks run off to hide?
Are they playing a game with pride?
Is my hairbrush in a secret feud?
Or just tangled up in morning crude?

What makes the chicken cross the road?
Is it to escape, or lighten the load?
Do toasters dream of fluffy bread?
Or do they just wish to be properly fed?

Why does the world spin like a top?
Does it ever think of taking a stop?
Are clouds really just cotton candy creations?
Or fashion statements in skyward rotations?

In a tornado where giggles collide,
Let's dance with the winds, our worries aside.
Embrace the zany in every curvy spin,
And find joy in chaos, where wonders begin.

The Horizon of Not Knowing

Why do pancakes flip with such flair?
Do they dream of syrup, or a wealthy bear?
Is the horizon just a line of intrigue?
Or a clever joke that makes us fatigue?

What makes clocks tick with such haste?
Are they counting moments, just for taste?
Do shadows argue about who gets the light?
Or do they just mingle until the night?

Why do whispers echo in empty rooms?
Are they the ghosts of our old silly dooms?
Do windows hold secrets of what they have seen?
Or do they just frame every day's routine?

As we walk toward what we can't define,
Let's laugh at the riddles, over a glass of wine.
For on this horizon, full of jest,
We find joy in questions, eternally blessed.

Gaze of the Inquisitive

Why is the sky so blue, oh friend?
And why do cats pretend to bend?
Do socks really disappear at night?
Or do they fly away in sheer delight?

Why do we never find a penny?
Or is it just a trick, too many?
If questions lead us on a spree,
Is the answer as simple as a cup of tea?

Where Certainty Meets Ambiguity

Why do we wear our shoes on our feet?
Could it be a fashion, or a tricky cheat?
If grass is green, then why not blue?
Life's strange palette, it's hard to pursue.

When is a door really a window?
Could it be just an overgrown bingo?
If the answers elude in a funny game,
Who knew confusion could bring such fame?

The Labyrinth of Wonder

What's the secret of a chicken's cluck?
Is it about fate, or just plain luck?
Why do we dodge the question arrays?
As though sanity wears a cap made of haze.

When does a puzzle become a snare?
Is it just my mind, laid out bare?
With twists and turns like a winding path,
Questions may lead to giggles and wrath.

Silent Queries on the Breeze

Why does the wind whisper my name?
Is it joking, or playing a silly game?
Do clouds drift 'cause they just don't care?
Do they giggle at us, standing there?

What makes the stars twinkle and play?
Are they laughing at us in dismay?
Though answers elude in a comical dance,
In this circus of questions, we twirl and prance.

The Mirror of Perpetual Wonder

Is that a bird or just a hat?
How did I lose my only cat?
I chase my thoughts like butterflies,
They laugh and dance beneath the skies.

Why does my coffee taste like shoe?
Are socks alive, or just askew?
I stand and ponder, scratch my head,
Did I leave the iron on instead?

What's the secret to that ice cream?
Is it just me or does it scream?
I make a list of all my dreams,
But then I lose it, or so it seems.

The clock is ticking, what's the time?
Is waking up just a silly rhyme?
With questions bouncing like a ball,
I trip and tumble, but have a ball.

The Elusive Nature of Knowing

The cat is plotting, or so it seems,
With tiny paws and grandiose dreams.
Why do we worry about the stars?
They surely must have better cars.

Is my sandwich talking back to me?
Do pickles have a philosophy?
I wonder if the sun gets tired,
Or if the moon is just inspired.

Should I wear purple? Or maybe red?
What's in this box? I'll check, instead.
I open it, and then I find,
Just another question on my mind.

Why did the chicken cross the street?
To ponder why it feels so sweet?
I laugh at all these quirky doubts,
And sketch my worries into shouts.

Threads of Endless Inquiry

What really is a universal truth?
Why does my wisdom look uncouth?
Is art just mess or messy art?
And who on earth invented tart?

I lost my keys beneath the couch,
Did they escape? Or just give out a grouch?
Each thread I pull leads to a knot,
Is thinking deep just overthought?

Can ice cream melt the moon away?
Why does the toaster want to play?
I watch my plants, they seem to grin,
Do they hold secrets deep within?

Why do Mondays feel like clowns?
They juggle frowns and wear sad crowns.
With every question, laughter spills,
I'm chasing joy through life's odd thrills.

Echoes in the Chasm of Silence

What makes the leaves dance in the breeze?
Are flowers shy, ask for some cheese?
Why does the kettle whistle loud?
Is it singing sweetly to the crowd?

Do clouds have meetings to discuss,
Which shape they'll take, who blows the fuss?
I tiptoe softly through this thought,
In case the answers can be caught.

Should I talk to my lunch today?
Does it have opinions to convey?
Is that my burger rolling eyes,
Or just the ghost of clever fries?

What if socks chased all the shoes?
Would we all end up with the blues?
In endless quiet, I still pry,
And chuckle at the questions nigh.

The Sound of a Heart Asking

Why does toast always land down?
While cats just act like the crown.
Is the moon just cheese on a plate?
Or a funny joke that fell late?

Do buttons wish they were a thread?
Or do zippers want to be fed?
Do fish think they're in a parade?
Or just bored in their watery shade?

Are socks secretly in disguise?
Or planning a coup in the skies?
What do dogs whisper at night?
I bet it's tales of pure delight.

With every laugh, a question grows,
And yet, who really ever knows?
In the noise of a heart's own cheer,
Is the answer really standing near?

Fractured Reflections

Mirrors giggle with every glance,
Do they see a shadowy dance?
When I frown, do they crack a grin?
Or ponder the chaos within?

What's that strange fruit on my plate?
Could it be mocking my fate?
If time is money, where's the bank?
I bet that's where I fell off the plank.

Do clouds ever swap their shape?
Or play dress-up in vast drape?
If wishes float like papers in air,
Do they ever stop and just stare?

In the puddles of thoughts misplaced,
We find reflections, humor laced.
If laughter is truly the key,
Then what does it unlock, oh me?

The Boundless Openings of Curiosity

Why do ducks waddle like that?
Is it a strut or a chat?
Can turtles really take a break?
Or do they just move for their sake?

If sunflowers follow the sun,
Can they tell us how to have fun?
What's with the socks on the floor?
Are they a fashion statement or lore?

Do books ever argue with pens?
Or make peace before the end?
If laughter is measured in degrees,
Are puns just a form of tease?

When questions fill our wandering mind,
A treasure trove is what we'll find.
With every answer tucked in jest,
Each playful thought sparks joy, our quest.

A Canvas of Uncertainties

If paint could talk, what would it say?
Would it gossip about the fray?
Is blue feeling a bit too sad?
Or does red just want to be mad?

Why do socks always play hide and seek?
Is it possible they're just too chic?
If crayons dream of being a pen,
Do they hope it won't lead to a bend?

What does the wind sing to the trees?
Are they plotting world strategies?
If puddles laugh when it rains,
Are they hiding their playful grains?

With each splatter of color and cheer,
Questions dance in the atmosphere.
In the art of our clever debate,
Do we paint the questions or fate?

The Dance of Doubt

I twirl with my worries, they lead me around,
As I trip over answers that can't be found.
Do I wear my socks funny or is it just me?
The experts are clueless, just wait and see!

I ask the wise owl if I should wear shoes,
It blinks with confusion; what's there to lose?
My slippers are comfy, with holes in the toes,
But doubt's like a dance—nobody knows!

With each little question, a shimmy, a sway,
The more that I ponder, the more I'm led astray.
Should I bake or should I fry? What's on the menu?
Guess I'll just dance while my brain does a venue!

So I shuffle and giggle, let worry unwind,
For every odd query, a new jive I'll find.
As answers elude, I'll just prance in delight,
Embracing the chaos, my goofiest flight.

Questions in the Quiet

In the stillness of night, my thoughts come alive,
With questions a-plenty, oh how they thrive!
Is my cat really plotting or is it just me?
Can socks disappear like they've snuck out for tea?

Why do toast land butter-side down, with a frown?
And why must my plants always look like they drown?
Do chairs have feelings when we sit with a thud?
And does spaghetti dream of a big meatball flood?

I ponder the colors that fireflies wear,
And if clouds giggle when we complain about air.
What's the secret of trees, standing tall without doubt?
Do they laugh when the wind blows their leaves all about?

So in the quiet, questions dance like a bee,
Each query a tickle, a delectable spree.
While answers may hide like a shy little mouse,
I'll throw a wild party right here in my house!

Illusions of Certainty

I wake up each morning with plans set in stone,
Yet by afternoon, I'm lost and alone.
Like making pancakes, I sought the right mix,
But burnt the whole batch, oh, what a cruel fix!

Should I wear that old hat that's so out of style?
Or wrestle with fashion in a quirky new dial?
Each choice turns absurd, a game of charades,
Where certainty dances; it winks and it fades!

Should I buy a new plant or just let it be?
Then make it a pet, oh, the joy—wait and see!
With questions like circus tricks in my head,
I laugh as I wonder what lies up ahead.

But really, who knows where the path will unfold?
With fewer clear answers, more stories retold.
If answers are puzzles, I'll join in the fun,
With giggles and blunders, the day's just begun!

Voices of the Unspoken

In a crowded room, my thoughts play hide and seek,
Like whispers of secrets, they shyly speak.
Should I stretch for the chips or just take a chance?
Or dance like a dork, leading others to prance?

The unspoken voices, they giggle and snicker,
Mocking my choices, each thought growing thicker.
Do plants get lonely if I leave them alone?
Or do they thrive better when I'm on my phone?

What if the moon is just cheese on a plate?
Made for the mice who await their sweet fate?
And what's with the socks that never find pairs?
They rally in silence, plotting new wares!

So let's cheer for the questions that tickle the mind,
For the puzzle of answers we'll never quite find.
In the laughter of echoes we'll happily bask,
Embracing the wonders of every weird task!

Probings into the Infinite

Why do socks always go to hide?
Is there a hole in the universe, wide?
Is it a plot by laundry's evil spin?
Or just their way of trying to win?

How come the cat can stare so still?
Does she see secrets beyond our will?
Or is she plotting a grand escape?
With stolen snacks, her own little cape?

The toaster burns bread with such glee,
While you just wanted a simple tea.
Is it an artist, or a cruel prank?
That bread's a canvas, a toast-ful tank?

Do dreams reveal what's deep inside?
Or are they just rides on a joy-filled slide?
With unicorns or a dragon's snore,
Leaving you laughing, then wanting more?

Footprints in the Sand of Inquisition

Why do ducks always quack in rhyme?
Are they in theater, playing all the time?
Or just on a hunt for a earbud's prize,
Making up stories beneath sunny skies?

Why does ice cream always melt so fast?
Is it escaping from its glowing cast?
It drips and slides like a slippery fish,
While you just wanted to savor your wish!

Do mirrors show truths, or merely fakes?
Is my reflection crafting high-stakes?
Why does my hair choose days to act wild?
Is it a battle, or just nature's child?

Why do we humans forget our keys?
Are they hiding from us, if you please?
Maybe they're off on a grand holiday,
While we're left searching in disarray!

Silent Echoes of Uncertainty

Why do squirrels always chatter on?
Can they see futures while we yawn?
Are they discussing the world's next scheme?
Or just debating which tree's the dream?

Why do we laugh when we trip and fall?
Is our body trying to teach us all?
That awkward moments can steal the show,
With a belly laugh as the best throw?

Why do plants seem to droop and pout?
Are they waiting for us to find them out?
Do they have gossip, or secrets to tell?
Or just need water? Oh, what the hell?

Why do we search for meaning so far?
Is it hiding 'neath a tree or a star?
Perhaps it's just like a playful breeze,
Tickling thoughts with gentle tease!

Whispers in the Wind

Why do pigeons always look so proud?
Are they the kings of the bustling crowd?
Strutting around with their chest held high,
While we just wonder, oh me, oh my?

Why do we ponder on things so strange?
Like why do bananas sometimes arrange?
In a way that makes us laugh and cheer,
Are they comedians hiding in here?

Why does the fridge hum a sleepy tune?
Is it dreaming of tacos, or maybe a spoon?
While we open it, hoping for snacks,
Only to find leftovers in weird packs?

Why do we ask why, again and again?
Is it a quest that will never have zen?
But in all the questions and giggling grace,
We find funny moments fill empty space!

Autumn Leaves of Uncertainty

Falling leaves dance in the air,
Whispering secrets, none seem fair.
Do they know where they're going next?
Or are they just a little perplexed?

Squirrels ponder their nutty stash,
While I question if money can clash.
Do acorns dream of becoming trees?
Or is their fate just a winter's freeze?

Clouds float by with a chuckle too,
They'll bring the rain, but when? Who knew?
With umbrellas upside down in glee,
It's a mystery for you and me!

But as the chill finds its way inside,
I laugh at the absurdity I can't hide.
For in this madness, we take our stand,
With humor guiding this chaotic land.

Traces of What Remains Unsaid

Words linger like a faint perfume,
Around us they hover, like reading the room.
Why did I say it, why did I not?
Did he get it? Or just forgot?

Dinner guests with their knowing smiles,
Conversations filled with missing miles.
What did you mean when you looked that way?
Was it time to laugh, or time to sway?

The cat ignores all my queries loud,
With a flick of her tail, she's quite proud.
Does she know why I'm feeling this way?
Or is she just waiting for me to play?

And so here I sit with riddles untold,
Laughing at thoughts that never get bold.
In the silence, a chuckle creeps near,
Perhaps it's better to simply just cheer!

Dreams Painted in Shades of Ambivalence

In a world where visions blur and blend,
I question if they're real or pretend.
Are those unicorns or just my bed sheets?
And why do I always find talking sweets?

Midnight snacks give philosophical scowls,
Chips whisper secrets, making me howl.
Do nachos know their cheesy fate?
Or are they just waiting for something great?

Colors swirl in a whimsical haze,
Dancing like socks lost in a maze.
What is the meaning behind this choice?
Should I paint it pink or hear the voice?

Yet here I stand, brush in my grip,
Contemplating this curious trip.
With every stumble an artistic gain,
I laugh at the chaos, it's all in the brain!

The Searcher's Lament

With a map and a coffee, I search high and low,
For answers that dance just out of toe.
Do the stars hide in yesterday's fridge?
Or am I just building a silly little bridge?

Looking under cushions and in corners tight,
Finding only dog hair and a light.
Do keys have a party whenever I'm lost?
Or is this a game that they love at all cost?

I've tried to Google the meaning of things,
But the internet offers up only slings.
Does wisdom come from a cereal box?
Or just from the silence of wise old fox?

Yet here I am with a grin on my face,
Enjoying this frantic, hilarious race.
For in every question that circles my head,
Lies the fun of the journey, the joy to be led!

The Quest for Elusive Answers

Why is the sky so wide and blue?
Cows wear bells, but do they sing too?
What makes socks vanish in the wash?
Is, 'What's for dinner?' just a cosmic swosh?

Oh, I ponder while eating my toast,
About the unicorns that I love the most.
Are there answers hiding in the fridge?
Or perhaps they're lurking under the bridge?

Do fish get thirsty, or just pretend?
Is my cat the true boss, or just a friend?
If ducks can quack, why not a turtle?
Each thought's a gem in an absurd circle.

So I wander with questions like floating balloons,
Chasing for answers at high noon.
With laughter echoing all around,
In this zany quest, what have I found?

The Silence Between Thoughts

In silence where thoughts come to play,
They dance around in a comical way.
Do ants really plan world domination?
Or are they just on a food vacation?

Why do we park in a driveway so wide,
But drive on a parkway, oh where's the guide?
Are cookies better with sprinkles or sprout?
A thought's just a seed, twist it about!

Why do we sneeze when we smell the spring?
Do robots dream of electronic bling?
In the quiet between, all questions arise,
With chuckles and giggles, oh what a surprise!

So here's to the wonder that tickles the brain,
In this quirky silence, we're all quite insane.
As laughter erupts, we start to muse,
In the land of the puzzled, there's nothing to lose!

Eclipsed Realities

I ponder the moon when it plays hide and seek,
Does it know it's bright, or is it just sleek?
If shadows could talk, what tales would they tell?
Would they laugh at the stumbles or ring a bright bell?

What's the point of a rubber band ball?
Is it just for fun or a plan to enthrall?
If a tree falls and nobody's near,
Does it really make a sound, or just disappear?

Oh, I wonder about socks, where do they flee?
Maybe they join a circus on a grand spree.
Do stars gossip, twinkling in their clumps?
Or are they just blushing after all those jumps?

In these eclipsed moments, I sit and I muse,
With realities bending, there's little to lose.
As I chuckle at thoughts that swirl in my head,
In this topsy-turvy world, I'll dance instead!

A Garden of Potential Questions

In my garden of thoughts, questions bloom bright,
Do cucumbers ever dream of a night flight?
Why do tomatoes never play hide and seek?
Are they too proud, or just too meek?

Why does the scarecrow keep standing so tall?
Is he waiting for wisdom to grace him with a call?
Do carrots hum when they're snug in the dirt?
Or is it just worms that are flinging the hurt?

Could peas in a pod plot a grand scheme?
Or are they content just to float in a dream?
If flowers could talk, would they scream in delight?
A world full of wonders, oh what a sight!

So I stroll through the garden, with laughter in bloom,
Where questions are flowers, and giggles consume.
With every new thought that springs up anew,
In this vibrant patch, there's always a clue!

The Curiosity of Dawn

The rooster crows, but why so loud?
Is he a bard or just too proud?
The sun peeks in with a cheeky grin,
As if it knows where the day begins.

Questions rise like steam from tea,
Why do we park in driveways, you see?
The cat just yawns, unbothered by fate,
As we ponder over breakfast plate.

Birds tweet messages, but what do they say?
Are they gossiping or just here to play?
As the morning dances with silly prance,
We sip our doubts in a caffeinated trance.

Watching shadows stretch and sway,
Are they nightmares, or just here to stay?
With giggles sparked by thoughts unclear,
We embrace the whimsy with hearty cheer.

Shadows of Unresolved

In the corner sits a sock, so lone,
It asks itself, 'Is this my home?'
With mismatched shoes lined up in rows,
Who's to say where each one goes?

I ponder mysteries like 'What's that smell?'
Maybe last night's dinner has a story to tell?
A goldfish stares, with those curious eyes,
Perhaps he knows what lies in the skies.

Light bulbs flicker as I scratch my head,
Do they dream of being turned off instead?
As shadows dance, the clock ticks loud,
"Why is the sun still hiding behind a cloud?"

Kitchen utensils mock my plight,
Are they plotting when I turn out the light?
With every riddle, we laugh till we cry,
Perhaps the answers are just meant to lie.

Unraveled Threads of Existence

A tangled yarn rests beneath the chair,
What stories does it hide with flair?
Knitting needles sit, too shy to chat,
Wondering if they're meant for a cat.

Why do cookies crumble when they laugh?
Is milk the secret behind their gaff?
As crumbs collect, they form a trail,
Leading us on a quest to unveil.

Mirrors reflect back questions galore,
"Who's that stranger? I'm not so sure."
With every glance, I stare in disbelief,
"What's beneath this smile? Is it grief?"

In a world so keen on telling tales,
Penguins in tuxedos, with no sales,
We dance in circles, chasing our thoughts,
With giggles and winks, that's how we're caught.

Paradoxes of the Heart

I bought a heart-shaped box of pain,
Is it for candy or a love disdain?
Wrapped in ribbons of endless chatter,
Confusion reigns in every pitter patter.

Why do we laugh when we are sad?
Is it to mask what we never had?
The jokes we tell, a bittersweet art,
A laugh tracks laughter that breaks the heart.

Why do ducks quack without a care?
Are they sharing secrets, unaware?
As we walk on roads of twist and turn,
We trip on questions, but never learn.

In this circus of whims and vague designs,
We juggle thoughts as we sip on wines,
With heart-shaped boxes we carry our load,
And find the fun in this winding road.

The Unanswered Horizon

Why does toast always land down?
I toss, it spins, then hits the ground.
Is butter a guardian of fate?
Or does it just love to debate?

Socks vanish into the great blue,
Is there a portal? Do they feel woo?
Cats stare at walls like they're wise,
What secrets hide in their feline eyes?

Why can't we find the remote right?
It hides like it's playing a prank tonight.
And why does the fridge hum and sigh?
Is it gossiping about the pie?

With each little riddle I ponder,
I can't help but laugh and just wander.
The universe spins like a disco ball,
Is it laughing at me after all?

Musings of a Restless Soul

Why are we drawn to the skies?
Are clouds just shy or really wise?
Do trees gossip on windy days?
Or do they just sway in a daze?

Why do we like socks that don't match?
Is fashion's code just a bad catch?
Do dreams come with a manual guide?
Or are we lost on this fun ride?

Why do ducks waddle and quack so loud?
Are they leaders of an unseen crowd?
When will my phone stop being sly?
Why do apps crash? Oh my, oh my!

The mind is a curious thing indeed,
Chasing answers like a golden bead.
With giggles and grins in the quest,
I'll dance through questions, that's the best!

Echoes of an Unwritten Chapter

What's lurking in the shadowed nook?
A dusty book or a sly crook?
Why do we wonder about the moon?
Is it a friend or just a cartoon?

Do socks have feelings when we lose them?
Or are they off on a journey, unseen?
How come my plants never give hints?
Do they judge me for my bad prints?

What's the deal with cereal and milk?
Is there magic there, or just silk?
Why does my phone always need a charge?
Is it plotting to turn my day large?

As I scribble down these silly lines,
I laugh at each thought that intertwines.
In this jumbled, whimsical quest,
I find joy in riddles; it's the best!

The Infinite Loop of Wonder

Where does the sun go at night?
Does it tuck itself in, snug and tight?
Do stars play hide and seek with us?
Or are they just full of cosmic fuss?

Why do we crave ice cream in winter?
Is that a trend that just won't splinter?
What wakes up the snoozing alarm?
Is it pulling a prank, or just charm?

Why do they call it fast food?
When I'm still waiting, feeling crude?
Do pens run away when I'm in need?
Or do they plot like they're on a steed?

In this dance of questions, I sway,
Wondering why clouds float in play.
With laughter and quirks, I shall stroll,
For answers aren't the main goal at all!

Tides of Perpetual Wonder

Why is the sky blue, not green or brown?
Do fish wear their scales like a fancy gown?
If cows could drive, where would they go?
Can plants hear gossip whispered low?

What makes a sandwich the best of its kind?
Is it secret sauce or just being kind?
Do shadows leave home when the sun goes down?
Or do they party and dance all around?

Where do the lost socks go, to have fun?
Do they play bingo till the day is done?
If you tickle a pickle, will it laugh out loud?
Or just roll away, feeling quite proud?

Can a cat play chess, or just nap on the board?
Are pigeons plotting? Oh, I can't afford!
Why does the cookie taste better when warm?
Is it just magic, or a secret charm?

Reflections in a Shattered Mirror

Am I quirky or just a little odd?
Can I blame my reflection or give it a nod?
If I sing in the shower, does the shampoo clap?
And do my towels gossip about my mishap?

If mirrors crack, do they start to confide?
Sharing their tales about what they've spied?
What if I asked my shoes where they've been?
Would they tell stories, or would they just grin?

When I trip over air, is it just my fate?
Or a prank from the universe, destined to wait?
What do the clouds think of all this fuss?
Do they chuckle and say, "What's the rush?"

Do eyebrows raise like alerting alarms?
When I dance like a chicken, causing charms?
If laughter's the answer, what's the big query?
It must be the joy that keeps us all cheery!

The Unwritten Pages of Tomorrow

What will tomorrow bring, a dance or a frown?
Should I take the bus or just twirl around?
If I wrote my plans on a fluffy cloud,
Will it float away, feeling so proud?

Do stars giggle when night starts to spread?
Or do they just roll their eyes instead?
What if the moon, on its silver throne,
Is just an old man, feeling alone?

Can I teach a tomato to do the cha-cha?
Would it join me, or laugh like a llama?
If my toes could talk, what tales would they tell?
Would they reminisce or just wish me well?

If dust bunnies hold secret parties at night,
Do they play hide and seek till morning light?
What's the recipe for a giggle or two?
Just sprinkle some joy, with a dash of you!

Questions Like Stars in the Night

Why do ducks waddle, not walk like a pro?
Do they ponder the cosmos or just go with the flow?
If I ask a volcano, will it explode with glee?
Or will it just grumble and sip its tea?

When cats sit like royalty, what do they think?
Are they plotting world peace or just needing a wink?
If I gave my goldfish a crash course in flight,
Would it soar through the air, creating delight?

Do rainbows giggle when they arch in the sky?
Or is that laughter just a sweet little sigh?
What if the sun had its own little game?
Would it play hide and seek, never the same?

If every lost thought comes back with a twist,
Would we dance with them all, in a glittery mist?
Questions like stars twinkle bright in my mind,
Leaving me curious, and joyfully blind!

When Days Do Not Conclude

The sun sets low, yet dawn's still near,
Do we sip our tea or chug our beer?
A squirrel in a hat gives a puzzled glance,
As if to say, "Is this all just chance?"

We've got laundry waiting, what's on the list?
Oh wait, it's gone! Did it cease to exist?
A mystery wrapped in a towel's fold,
Did we buy socks or secrets untold?

The clock on the wall tick-tocks in jest,
Might it be time for a wiggly rest?
With bananas on phone and fish in a stew,
Who knows what chaos might next ensue?

Each day is a dance, a whimsical spree,
Chasing our tails, as silly as can be.
With giggles and grumbles, we twirl and we spin,
At the end of it all, where do we begin?

Heartbeats of Immaculate Doubt

A clock says tick but means tock,
Does it really care? Or just want to mock?
If cheese could talk, what tales would it tell?
After all, isn't that just a wish on a shell?

The cat winks slyly, as if in on a plot,
Is it breakfast time, or have we forgot?
A parrot squawks truths that rattle and roll,
Within its bright feathers lies wisdom untold.

Questioning sandwiches whilst munching away,
"Why doesn't toast come with more things to say?"
Tickling the thoughts that swirl in my head,
Maybe answers are snacks better left spread.

In a riddle wrapped tightly in gummy bears,
Swirling around like our fanciful flares.
Each heartbeat giggles, as doubts jog along,
Creating a melody, whimsical song.

Mists of Intrigue

Under the fog where the lamposts blink,
Do shadows conspire or just sit and think?
A duck in a trench coat steps lightly aside,
What's cooking tonight? A conspiracy fried?

The streets whisper secrets in flows of the breeze,
Or perhaps it's just gossips? A rumor that teases.
With croissants and crooks wearing hats oh so tall,
Is wandering lost the best path of all?

With giggles and jests floating up through the air,
The mists murmur softly, no one seems to care.
Like cookie crumbs scattered on thoughts that might crack,
We sift through our day, waiting for the next act.

But hidden within these enigmatic streams,
Are laughs and odd musings, resembling dreams.
So let's dance among mysteries, curious sprouts,
Where flavor's a puzzle while fun's still what shouts!

Beneath the Veil of Knowing

Under the blanket of stars in the night,
Why do we ponder on what's wrong or right?
A clown on a unicycle, with shoes that squeak loud,
Leaves us bemused amidst the chuckling crowd.

With thoughts that blend freely in whimsical hues,
Like socks gone missing, or odd-shaped shoes.
Does the moon giggle, or carry a frown?
Can humor be heavy, or light like a gown?

Questions on napkins, spilled drinks on the floor,
Tangled up thoughts, what could be in store?
Between hiccups and chuckles, conclusions might stir,
While laughter is a language that dreams prefer.

So we dance through the mist of uncertain delight,
With whimsy our guide, we drift through the night.
Beneath all the chaos, where wonders do dwell,
Perhaps that's the magic we all wish to tell.

Shadows Cast by Wonder

Beneath the moon's confused glare,
I ponder socks without a pair.
Why do birds fly in a line?
Is there a bird that draws the design?

With coffee beans, I brew my fate,
Yet every cup tastes like a mate.
Do plants grow if we talk all day?
Or just ignore what we have to say?

The Mirage of Clarity

In search of truth, I found a cat,
Who spoke in rhymes while wearing a hat.
Do fish play chess when no one's around?
Or just tell tales of dreams they found?

With every riddle, I scratch my head,
Imagining toast that's perfectly spread.
Are clouds just cotton candy in disguise?
Are we just ants with giant wise eyes?

Question Marks in the Twilight

Why do donuts always taste so round?
And why's the moon so far and profound?
Do unicorns cry when they lose a race?
Or just gallop off, leaving no trace?

As shadows grow long, I seek and I seek,
What does the owl mean when it starts to peek?
How does a ninja's silence compare,
To a taco's crunch in the crisp evening air?

Flickering Flames of Inquiry

My candle flickers, asking me why,
Do stars always twinkle when I say goodbye?
If I plan a trip to the cheese-filled moon,
Will there be rats dancing to a tune?

As questions flutter like leaves in the breeze,
I ponder if jellybeans can sneeze.
Can rainbows giggle when they're seen from afar?
Or is that just how they raise the bar?

In Search of Missing Pieces

Where's my sock? I have just one,
This puzzle seems no longer fun.
My keys were here, they've made a run,
Oh, search begins, oh what a pun!

My coffee's cold, I sip with glee,
Wondering where all my thoughts flee.
Did I leave the stove? Oh wait, let me!
I think I've lost my sanity!

My cat is napping, dreaming bright,
Perhaps she's lost her own insight.
Should I check again? It feels so right,
Or join her in this silly plight?

It's all a game, a wibbly mess,
A chase for truth, it's anyone's guess.
Oh, missing pieces, please confess,
Just find my sock and end this stress!

Fleeting Glimpses of Clarity

In the shower, ideas flow,
Like soap bubbles, to and fro.
I grab a towel, but oh the woe,
What was that thought? I'll never know.

A fleeting glimpse, a spark, a tease,
Like wanting cheese, but it's just peas.
My mind's a maze, it never sees,
The point of all these memories.

Answers hide behind each corner,
Dancing away like a clown performer.
I chase them down, but they're much warmer,
Rich in laughter, yet far from former.

So let's embrace this goofy chase,
Laugh aloud, no time to waste.
For in confusion, there's a grace,
In every question, a smiling face.

The Abyss of a Thought

I ponder deep, then lose the thread,
What's for dinner? A crust of bread?
Forgot the laundry, it's all in my head,
This endless abyss where logic's dead.

Thoughts dive deep, like fish in blue,
Swirling round in circles, who knew?
Each time I pull one, it bids adieu,
Is that a dolphin? Or my old shoe?

I'm in a whirl, a dizzy spree,
Trying to grasp what's meant to be.
It slips right through, as fast as can be,
Oh look, a squirrel! So wild and free!

In this chasm, I can't quite see,
Answers trip and giggle with glee.
So onward I drift, just me and my tea,
Finding magic in every mystery.

Puzzles of a Fleeting Mind

A jumble of thoughts, like bits of yarn,
Twisted and tangled, causing alarm.
I search for peace, but where's the charm?
This puzzle seems intent to disarm.

My brain's a maze of jiggly bits,
Each path I take leads to funny skits.
Am I on stage? Or merely in fits?
Why did I walk in here with no wits?

Questions pop, like popcorn in air,
Each kernel a thought, none seem quite fair.
I laugh aloud, for I do declare,
All these riddles are too much to bear.

So here I stand, in this playful land,
Piecing together what slips from my hand.
With every giggle, I make my stand,
In this puzzle, I'm perfectly planned!

Whispers of an Unanswered Dawn

Morning's sun peeks through the haze,
Chasing sleep from its cozy maze.
Why does toast always land with a thud?
And socks vanish like they're made of mud?

Coffee spills with a rebellious cheer,
Who taught the cat to be a cavalier?
The clock ticks on with a cheeky grin,
As I ponder where my keys have been.

Birds chirp songs of a lost refrain,
Do they gossip of my unkempt mane?
With mismatched shoes I shuffle along,
Whispers of doubt in the morning song.

Yet laughter bubbles with every guess,
In this circus of colorful mess.
For questions abound like confetti in air,
While the answers snooze without a care.

The Echoes of Curiosity

Questions bounce like a rubber ball,
Do fish in the sea have a waterfall?
Why does cheese smell like old gym shoes?
And why do I still have so many blues?

The sky's a puzzle, lost in its blue,
Why do seagulls always steal my food?
The sun waves bye as the night takes the stage,
While I'm left to ponder this curious age.

I wonder if rocks get tired of being still,
And do clouds ever tire of their fluffy thrill?
The world's a riddle wrapped in a jest,
With answers that laugh, leaving me perplexed.

Yet in the chaos, a chuckle resides,
For questions alone are this fun ride.
So let's dance with our doubts, take a spin,
And embrace the whimsy that lives within.

Soliloquy of the Unsought

An apple a day, if only it knew,
Why it must roll when I bring it to chew?
The remote's missing, it's played a grand game,
I swear I had it, this isn't the same.

Why do dogs chase their own wagging tail?
And whispers of pigeons script shadowy tales?
Each question a twist, like a noodle in soup,
While I'm left here, living in this loop.

Pants with holes, they're not on the list,
Yet zeros in pockets persist in their mist.
A mirror reflects a curious spark,
While the fridge hums secrets deep in the dark.

Still laughter rises like pies in the sky,
With every strange wonder I bare my sigh.
For in this riddle, I juggle the jest,
And find in the awkward, I'm subtly blessed.

Searching Shadows in the Abyss

Why do shadows play hide and seek?
In corners they linger, too shy to speak.
The coffee's cold, yet I hear it snicker,
While time ticks on, just a little quicker.

Do dreams wear pajamas or dress up in stars?
And will socks from the dryer escape to Mars?
Life's little puzzles, all wrapped up in cheer,
Each day's a circus, but the clowns are near.

Why do we worry about things unseen?
Like my plants, they pretend to glean.
With dust bunnies forming a family tree,
I wonder if they have quirks like me.

Yet joy bubbles forth from the chaos we find,
In the questions that dance, ever intertwined.
So let's laugh in the dark and twirl in the light,
For unanswered moments make everything bright.

Chasing Fleeting Answers

Why is the sky blue, is that a joke?
Did the clouds forget to wear their cloak?
I asked a squirrel, he just twitched his tail,
He buried my question, leaving no trail.

If I chase the wind, will it say my name?
Or laugh at me, like it's all just a game?
I pondered deep while I walked on a street,
Hoping to find answers at my own two feet.

I held a shell up to hear the sea,
But all it told me was, 'Just let it be!'
The sun tickled my thoughts, then slipped away,
I chased shadows as they began to play.

With a giggle, I put my thoughts to rest,
Turns out the riddles would never be guessed.
But isn't it fun to just dance in the dark?
Even if answers are left in the park?

Unraveled Threads of Being

I knit my questions with yarn of dismay,
Each stitch a wonder, but they fray every day.
I ask the cat, who shrugs with sly grace,
He says, 'Just nap, it's a puzzling race!'

Why do socks vanish, do they jump out in cheer?
Are they off to a party, or just disappear?
My tea leaves have stories, but don't talk to me,
They swirl in patterns, as vague as can be.

In the mirror, reflections dance round and round,
But what is the truth? Is it lost, never found?
I tilt my hat to the curious stars,
They wink back with secrets from Jupiter, Mars.

Yet in this chaos, I find a small laugh,
Mismatched answers float on a whimsical raft.
So I'll embrace the mess, the unspooled thread,
For joy is the answer that's always unsaid.

The Puzzle of Existence

If I'm a puzzle, what's missing, you say?
Maybe the corner piece ran off for a play.
A jigsaw of thoughts scattered on the floor,
Each piece a giggle, but still wanting more.

The edges are crisp, with colors so bright,
But inside, oh dear, it's a wild fright!
A dog stares puzzled while tilting his head,
Is it a puzzle, or just thoughts in my bed?

I wrangle my questions like cats on the loose,
They chase my attention and tread on my muse.
Do ducks wear shoes? What's with the drums?
I laugh at the wisdom that chaos becomes.

In this mad jumble, I pluck at my strings,
Maybe confusion just needs some new wings.
So here's to the pieces, though some may be lost,
It's the giggle in seeking that counts the most.

In the Garden of Unknowns

In a garden of unknowns, I wander and peek,
What's that flower? Shall I dare to speak?
A butterfly giggles, says, 'Try asking me!'
But it flutters away, just too wild and free.

The sunflowers whisper of secrets untold,
They dance with the breeze, cheeky and bold.
I tickle the petals, and they sigh with glee,
'Questions are tasty, come munch them with tea!'

A frog on a lily croaks riddles aloud,
Its voice is a puzzle, mysterious and proud.
If frogs write poetry, what rhymes do they choose?
I jot down some thoughts, though I might just lose.

In this garden of giggles and playful delights,
Where questions bloom wildly under soft lights,
I'll be a curious bee, buzzing round like a fool,
For the joy of the search is its own golden rule.

www.ingramcontent.com/pod-product-compliance
Lightning Source LLC
Chambersburg PA
CBHW071834160426
43209CB00003B/298